THE COMPLETE PLANT BASED DIET COOKBOOK 2021

The Most complete cookbook guide to energize your body, lose weight fast and regain confidence. Lose up to 7 pounds in 7 days with simple and clear instructions.

Ursa Males

TABLE OF CONTENTS

BREAKFAST

1. Tasty Nut Packed Porridge

Preparation time: 10 minutes

Cooking time: 15 minutes

Servings: 4

Ingredients:

- 1 cup cashew nuts, raw and unsalted
- 1 cup pecans, halved
- 2 tablespoons Stevia
- 4 teaspoons coconut oil, melted
- 2 cups of water

Directions:

1. Slice the nuts in a food processor and form a smooth paste. Add water, oil, Stevia to the nut paste and transfer the mix to a saucepan.
2. Stir cook for 5 minutes on high heat. Reduce heat to low and simmer for 10 minutes. Serve warm and enjoy!

Nutrition: Calories: 260 Fat: 22g Carbohydrates: 12g Protein: 6g

2. Original Garlic Toast

Preparation time: 5 minutes

Cooking time: 5 minutes

Servings: 4

Ingredients:

- 1 teaspoon coconut oil
- Pinch of salt
- 1-2 teaspoons nutritional yeast
- 1 small garlic clove, pressed
- 1 slice wholegrain bread

Directions:

1. Take a small-sized bowl and add all ingredients except bread; mix well. Toast your bread with seasoned oil or use a toaster; it should take about 5 minutes
2. Once done, spread garlic mixes all over toast and serve. Enjoy!

Nutrition: Calories: 120 Fat: 6g Carbohydrates: 16g Protein: 7g

3. Gingerbread Waffles

Preparation Time: 30 minutes

Cooking Time: 20 minutes

Servings: 6

Ingredients:

- 1 cup spelt flour
- 2 teaspoon baking powder
- ¼ teaspoon salt
- 1 tablespoon ground flax seeds
- 1 ½ teaspoon ground cinnamon
- 2 teaspoon ground ginger
- 4 tablespoon coconut sugar
- ¼ teaspoon baking soda
- 1½ tablespoon olive oil
- 1 cup non-dairy milk
- 1 tablespoon apple cider vinegar
- 2 tablespoons blackstrap molasses

Directions:

1. Take a waffle iron, oil generously, and preheat. Take a large bowl and add the dry ingredients. Stir well together.

2. Put the wet ingredients into another bowl and stir until combined. Stir the dry and wet together until combined.
3. Pour the mixture into the waffle iron and cook at a medium temperature for 20 minutes. Open carefully and remove. Serve and enjoy.

Nutrition: Calories: 173 Fat: 5g Carbs: 29g Protein: 3g

4. Blueberry French Toast Breakfast Muffins

Preparation Time: 20 minutes

Cooking Time: 25 minutes

Servings: 12

Ingredients:

- 1 cup unsweetened plant milk
- 1 tablespoon ground flaxseed
- 1 tablespoon almond meal
- 1 tablespoon maple syrup
- 1 teaspoon vanilla extract
- 1 teaspoon cinnamon
- 2 teaspoons nutritional yeast
- ¾ cup frozen blueberries
- 9 slices soft bread
- ¼ cup oats
- 1/3 cup raw pecans
- ¼ cup of coconut sugar
- 3 tablespoons coconut butter, at room temperature
- 1/8 teaspoon sea salt
- 9 slices bread, each cut into 4

Directions:

1. Preheat your oven to 370°F and grease a muffin tin. Pop to one side. Find a medium bowl and add the

flaxseeds, almond meal, nutritional yeast, maple syrup, milk, vanilla, and cinnamon.

2. Mix well using a fork, then pop into the fridge. Grab your food processor and add the topping ingredients (except the coconut butter.) Whizz to combine.

3. Add the butter, then whizz again. Grab your muffin tin and add a teaspoon of the flax and cinnamon batter to the bottom of each space.

4. Add a square of the bread, then top with 5-6 blueberries. Sprinkle with 2 teaspoons of the crumble, then top with another piece of bread.

5. Place 5-6 more blueberries over the bread, sprinkle with more of the topping, then add the other piece of bread.

6. Add a tablespoon of the flax and cinnamon mixture on top and add a couple of blueberries on the top.

7. Pop into the oven and cook for 20-25 minutes until the top begins to brown. Serve and enjoy.

Nutrition: Calories: 132g Fat: 5g Carbs: 14g Protein: 3g

5. <u>Greek Garbanzo Beans on Toast</u>

Preparation Time: 25 minutes

Cooking Time: 5 minutes

Servings: 2

Ingredients:

- 2 tablespoons olive oil
- 3 small shallots, finely diced
- 2 large garlic cloves, finely diced
- ¼ teaspoon smoked paprika
- ½ teaspoon sweet paprika
- ½ teaspoon cinnamon
- ½ teaspoon salt
- ½-1 teaspoon sugar, to taste
- Black pepper, to taste
- 1 x 14oz. can peel plum tomatoes
- 2 cups cooked garbanzo beans
- 4-6 slices of crusty bread, toasted
- Fresh parsley and dill
- Pitted Kalamata olives

Directions:

1. Pop a skillet over medium heat and add the oil. Add the shallots to the pan and cook for five minutes. Add the

garlic and cook until ready, then add the other spices to the pan.

2. Stir well, then add the tomatoes. Lower the heat and simmer on low until the sauce thickens. Add the garbanzo beans and warm through. Season with sugar, salt, and pepper, then serve and enjoy.

Nutrition: Calories: 709g Fat: 12g Carbs: 23g Protein: 19g

6. <u>Fluffy Garbanzo Bean Omelet</u>

Preparation Time: 5 minutes

Cooking Time: 12 minutes

Servings: 1

Ingredients:

- ¼ cup besan flour
- 1 tablespoon nutritional yeast
- ½ teaspoon baking power
- ¼ teaspoon turmeric
- ½ teaspoon chopped chives
- ¼ teaspoon garlic powder
- 1/8 teaspoon black pepper
- ½ teaspoon Ener-G egg replacer
- ¼ cup + 1 tablespoon water
- Leafy greens, torn with hands
- Veggies
- Salsa
- Ketchup
- Hot sauce
- Parsley

Directions:

1. Grab a medium bowl and combine all the ingredients except the greens and veggies. Leave to stand for five

minutes. Place a skillet over medium heat and add the oil.

2. Pour the batter into the pan, spread, and cook for 3-5 minutes until the edges pull away from the pan. Add the greens and the veggies of your choice, then fold the omelet over.

3. Cook for 2 more minutes than pop onto a plate. Serve with the topping of your choice. Serve and enjoy.

Nutrition: Calories: 439 Fat: 8g Carbs: 35g Protein: 12g

7. Easy Hummus Toast

Preparation Time: 10 minutes

Cooking Time: 10 minutes

Servings: 1

Ingredients:

- 2 slices of sprouted wheat bread
- ¼ cup hummus
- 1 tablespoon hemp seeds
- 1 tablespoon roasted unsalted sunflower seeds

Directions:

1. Start by toasting your bread. Top with the hummus and seeds, then eat!

Nutrition: Calories: 316 Fat: 16g Carbs: 13g Protein: 18g

LUNCH

8. <u>Taco Salad</u>

Preparation Time: 10 Minutes

Cooking Time: 30 Minutes

Servings: 2

Ingredients:

- For the taco meat:
- ½ cup Walnuts, soaked for few hours
- ½ tsp. Cumin Powder
- 1 ½ tsp. Chili Powder
- Sea Salt, as needed
- Cayenne Pepper, as needed

- For the cashew cream:
- 1 cup Cashews, soaked for few hours
- 3 tbsp. Lemon Juice
- 12 tbsp. Water
- Sea Salt, as needed
- For the guacamole:
- 1 Avocado, large & ripe
- ½ tsp. Cumin, grounded
- ¼ cup Red Onion, chopped
- Sea Salt, as needed
- ½ of 1 Tomato, small
- 1 tbsp. + 1 tsp. Lemon Juice
- For salad:
- Salad Greens, as needed
- Salsa, as needed

Directions:

1. First, for the taco meat, place all the ingredients in a high-speed blender and pulse them for 20 to 25 seconds or until combined.
2. After that, blend the sauce ingredients in the blender and blend until you get a smooth and creamy sauce.
3. Then, with a fork, mash the avocado in a bowl and, once mashed, stir in the guacamole's remaining ingredients. Mix well.

4. Finally, to serve, place the salad greens on the bottom. On to it top place ¼ of the guacamole in the center.

5. Then, add salsa and half of the taco meat. Pipe the cashew cream over the taco meat. Garnish with green onions if desired.

Nutrition: Calories: 608 Proteins: 11g Carbohydrates: 18g Fat: 59.8g

9. <u>Black Bean Chili</u>

Preparation Time: 10 Minutes

Cooking Time: 30 Minutes

Servings: 6

Ingredients:

- 2 Sweet Potatoes, small & chopped
- 2 Garlic cloves, minced
- 15 oz. Diced Tomatoes
- 1 Onion, small & diced
- 1 tbsp. Chili Powder
- 2 tbsp. Olive Oil
- 15 oz. Black Beans
- 2 Carrots, medium & sliced
- ½ tsp. Garlic Powder
- ½ cup Vegetable Broth
- ¼ tsp. Black Pepper
- 1 tsp. Cumin
- ½ tsp. Salt
- ½ tsp. Cayenne

Directions:

1. First, heat oil in a Dutch oven over medium-high heat. Once the oil becomes hot, stir in the onion and garlic. Mix.

2. Cook them for 3 to 4 minutes or until softened. After that, stir in the sweet potato and carrots to it. Combine.

3. Continue cooking the sweet potato-onion mixture for another 5 minutes or until the veggies soften. Now, lower the heat to low and stir in all the remaining ingredients to the Dutch oven.

4. Give a good stir and cover it partially. Allow it to simmer for 23 to 25 minutes or until everything is cooked. Serve it hot.

Nutrition: Calories: 384 Proteins: 19g Carbohydrates: 67g Fat: 6g

10. Mexican Vegan Casserole

Preparation Time: 10 Minutes

Cooking Time: 30 Minutes

Servings: 8 to 10

Ingredients:

- 3 Tomatoes, chopped
- 1 ½ cups Red Bell Pepper, chopped
- 2 cups Onion, fresh
- ¾ cup of Salsa
- 2 × 15 ¾ oz. Black Beans washed & drained
- Corn Tortillas, needed
- 2 cloves of garlic, minced
- 2 tsp. Cumin, grounded
- 2 cups Vegan Cheese

Directions:

1. For making this tasty casserole fare, preheat the oven to 350 F. After that, heat onion, cumin, pepper, salsa, garlic, and black beans in a large-sized saucepan over medium-high heat.
2. Now, allow the mixture to simmer for 3 to 5 minutes while stirring it frequently. Next, place the corn tortillas on the bottom of a baking casserole.

3. Spoon half the bean mixture over it and then with the vegan cheese. Continue the layering until all are used.
4. Finally, cover the baking dish with a lid and bake for 10 to 15 minutes. Garnish with tomatoes and salsa.

Nutrition: Calories: 595 Proteins: 19g Carbohydrates: 72g Fat: 21g

11. Avocado, Spinach, and Kale Soup

Preparation time: 10 minutes

Cooking time: 0 minutes

Servings: 4

Ingredients:

- 2 avocados, pitted, peeled, and cut in halves
- 4 cups vegetable stock
- 2 tablespoons cilantro, chopped
- Juice of 1 lime
- 1 teaspoon rosemary, dried
- ½ cup spinach leaves
- ½ cup kale, torn
- Salt and black pepper to the taste

Directions:

1. In a blender, combine the avocados with the stock and the other ingredients, pulse well, divide into bowls and serve for lunch.

Nutrition: Calories 300 Fat 23g Carbs 6g Protein 7g

12. Curry Spinach Soup

Preparation time: 10 minutes

Cooking time: 0 minutes

Servings: 4

Ingredients:

- 1 cup almond milk
- 1 tablespoon green curry paste
- 1 pound spinach leaves
- 1 tablespoon cilantro, chopped
- Salt and black pepper to the taste
- 4 cups veggie stock
- 1 tablespoon cilantro, chopped

Directions:

1. In your blender, combine the almond milk with the curry paste and the other ingredients, pulse well, divide into bowls and serve for lunch.

Nutrition: Calories 240 Fat 4g Carbs 6g Protein 2g

13. Arugula and Artichokes Bowls

Preparation time: 5 minutes

Cooking time: 0 minutes

Servings: 4

Ingredients:

- 2 cups baby arugula
- ¼ cup walnuts, chopped
- 1 cup canned artichoke hearts, drained & quartered
- 1 tablespoon balsamic vinegar
- 2 tablespoons cilantro, chopped
- 2 tablespoons olive oil
- Salt and black pepper to the taste
- 1 tablespoon lemon juice

Directions:

1. Combine the artichokes with the arugula, walnuts, and the other ingredients in a bowl, toss, divide into smaller bowls and serve for lunch.

Nutrition: Calories 200 Fat 2g Carbs 5g Protein 7g

14. Minty Arugula Soup

Preparation time: 5 minutes

Cooking time: 10 minutes

Servings: 4

Ingredients:

- 3 scallions, chopped
- 1 tablespoon olive oil
- ½ Cup coconut milk
- 2 cups baby arugula
- 2 tablespoons mint, chopped
- 6 cups vegetable stock
- 2 tablespoons chives, chopped
- Salt and black pepper to the taste

Directions:

1. Heat-up a pot with the oil over medium-high heat, add the scallions, and sauté for 2 minutes. Add the rest of the ingredients, toss, bring to a simmer and cook over medium heat for 8 minutes more. Divide the soup into bowls and serve.

Nutrition: Calories 200 Fat 4g Carbs 6g Protein 10g

DINNER

15. Vegetable Alfredo

Preparation Time: 10 minutes

Cooking Time: 20 minutes

Servings: 4

Ingredients:

- 1 onion, chopped
- 1 orange bell pepper, chopped
- 1 red bell pepper, chopped
- 1 zucchini squash
- 1 summer squash
- 1 (12 oz.) container mushrooms

- ½ cup Brazil nut cheese sauce
- 1 (10 oz.) bag spelt tortellini pasta
- 1 tbsp. grapeseed oil
- Sea salt to taste
- 1 tsp. oregano
- 2 tbsp. chopped fresh basil
- 1 tsp. onion powder
- 1 tsp. cayenne pepper

Directions:

1. Cook the pasta according to package Directions. Chop the veggies and set aside. Add oil to a skillet and add the vegetables.
2. Season with herbs and seasonings and cook for 2 minutes. Add sauce and pasta. Mix and cook for 1 minute. Serve.

Nutrition: Calories: 371 Fat: 10g Carb: 56g Protein: 11g

16.   Sushi Roll-Ups

Preparation Time: 20 minutes

Cooking Time: 0 minutes

Servings: 2

Ingredients:

- For the dip/hummus:
- 1 fennel bulb
- A glug of olive oil
- 1 pinch of dried sage
- 1 tbsp. tahini
- A handful of almonds
- 3 ½ oz chickpeas from a can, drained
- Pinch salt
- Juice of ½ lemon
- For the Roll-Ups:
- 1 capsicum sliced into matchsticks
- 1 small bunch of cilantros
- 1 avocado, sliced
- 1 cucumber, cut into matchsticks
- 1 parsnip, cut into matchsticks
- 2 medium zucchinis

Directions:

1. Pulse all the Ingredients for the hummus in a blender. Add a bit of lemon and olive oil to get your desired consistency.
2. To make the roll-ups, first, chop the zucchini into long thin strips. Then lay individual zucchini strips out and spread a generous amount of almond hummus onto the zucchini strip.
3. Now add little amounts of the avocado, cucumber, and the matchsticks of veggies. Top with some sesame seeds, and then serve.

Nutrition: Calories: 743 Fat: 51g Carb: 50g Protein: 31g

17. Mushroom "Chicken Tenders"

Preparation Time: 1 hour

Cooking Time: 30 minutes

Servings: 6

Ingredients:

- Grapeseed oil as needed
- 1 tsp. ground cloves
- 1 tsp. cayenne powder
- 2 tsp. ginger powder
- 2 tsp. onion powder
- 2 tsp. sage
- 2 tsp sea salt
- 2 tsp. basil
- 2 tsp. oregano
- 1 ½ cup spelt flour
- 1 ½ cups spring flour
- 2 to 6 Portobello mushrooms

Directions:

1. Slice the mushrooms caps approximately half-inch apart. Add mushrooms, oil, water, and half of the individual seasonings to the bowl and mix for 1 hour.
2. In a separate bowl, blend the rest of the seasonings and the spelt flour and then batter the mushrooms.

3. Preheat oven to 400F. Grease a baking sheet with grapeseed oil and put the mushrooms on the baking sheet. Bake 15 minutes per side, or until crispy. Serve.

Nutrition: Calories: 276 Fat: 6.5g Carb: 49.48g Protein: 10.72g

18. Quinoa Pasta with Tomato Artichoke Sauce

Preparation Time: 10 minutes

Cooking Time: 20 minutes

Servings: 2

Ingredients:

- 2 tbsp extra-virgin olive oil
- 1 pinch cayenne pepper
- ½ tsp. sea salt
- 3 tbsp. basil, fresh
- 1 tsp. vegetable stock
- 1-ounce walnuts
- 1 fennel bulb
- 1 onion, chopped
- 8 ounces artichoke hearts
- 5 ounces cherry tomatoes, fresh
- 7 ounces quinoa or spelt pasta

Directions:

1. Cook the artichoke until tender. Then cook the pasta as stated in the package Directions. Chopped all the veggies.

2. Heat 2 tablespoons of oil and stir fry onions, nuts, and fennel for a few minutes. Then add the cooked artichokes and tomatoes and cook for 2 minutes.

3. Scoop about ½ cup of water and then dissolve the vegetable stock into the water. Add into a pan and simmer for 2 minutes on low heat. Stir regularly. Add basil, season with salt and pepper. Put the sauce on the pasta and serve.

Nutrition: Calories: 719 Fat: 26g Carb: 111g Protein: 23.9g

19. Alkalizing Tahini Noodle Bowl

Preparation Time: 10 minutes

Cooking Time: 0 minutes

Servings: 2

Ingredients:

- 1 tsp. black sesame seeds
- ½ avocado, chopped
- 2 green onions, chopped
- 4 kale, chopped
- 1 parsnip, shredded
- 4 leaves of romaine, chopped
- 1 yellow zucchini, spiralized
- Dressing:
- 1 tsp. agave
- 2 tbsp. lemon juice
- 1 tbsp. tahini
- Dash of salt

Directions:

1. Put all the vegetables you chopped in a bowl. Add all Ingredients for dressing in another bowl and whisk.

2. Pour the dressing over the vegetables and garnish with sesame seeds.

Nutrition: Calories: 209 Fat: 14.5g Carb: 22.07g Protein: 5.49g

20. Alkaline Meatloaf

Preparation Time: 15 minutes

Cooking Time: 70 minutes

Servings: 1 loaf

Ingredients:

- 1 cup prepared wild rice
- ½ cup homemade tomato sauce, divided
- ½ cup chopped yellow onion, divided
- ½ cup chopped green bell pepper, divided
- 1 shallot, chopped
- 2 cups mixed mushrooms, chopped
- ¼ tsp. cloves
- ½ tsp. ginger
- ½ tsp. tarragon
- 1 tsp. thyme
- 1 tsp. sage
- 1 tbsp. sea salt
- 1 tbsp. onion powder
- 1 cup garbanzo flour or spelt flour
- cups breadcrumbs (made of spelt flour)
- 2 cups cooked chickpeas
- Cayenne to taste

Directions:

1. Clean and dry wild rice. Prepare the chickpeas as well and set them aside. Mix garbanzo flour or spelt flour with bread crumbs and set the mixture aside.
2. Chop the green peppers and the onions and place half of each of them to the side.
3. Now chop the shallots and mushrooms and add them to a food processor, along with chickpeas, half of the onion, half of the green peppers, and spices.
4. Pulse the mixture until fully incorporated. Then add in 2 tbsp of tomato sauce and the wild rice. And continue to blend until a paste.
5. Move the mixture to a mixing bowl. Add the remaining flour, bread crumbs, onion, and green pepper. Mix well.
6. Pour the mixture into a greased pan and cover with the remaining tomato sauce—Bake in the preheated oven at 350F within 60 to 70 minutes. Cool, slice, and serve.

Nutrition: Calories: 265 Fat: 2.96g Carb: 48g Protein: 13.15g

21. Pizza

Preparation Time: 15 minutes

Cooking Time: 30 minutes

Servings: 6

Ingredients:

- For the crust:
- 1 ½ cups spelt flour
- 1 cup spring water
- ½ tsp onion powder
- ½ tsp oregano
- ½ tsp sea salt
- ½ tsp basil
- Cheese:
- ¼ tsp sea salt
- ½ tsp basil
- ½ tsp oregano
- ½ tsp. onion powder
- 1 tsp. lime juice
- ¼ cup hemp milk/nut milk
- ½ cup spring water
- 1 cup Brazil nuts, soaked overnight
- Toppings:
- Homemade tomato sauce as needed

- 3 tbsp. red onion chopped
- ½ plum tomato, sliced

Directions:

1. Combine all the seasonings in a bowl with spelt flour and then add in half a water cup. Add more water if needed.
2. Make a dough and roll on a floured surface, then place the dough into a baking sheet that is gently coated with oil. Poke holes with a fork.
3. Bake within 10 to 15 minutes in the preheated oven at 350F. Meanwhile, add all Ingredients for cheese in a blender and process until smooth.
4. Once the crust is cooked, coat it with the cheese, sauce, and toppings. Bake again in the bottom rack at 425F for 10 to 15 minutes more. Enjoy.

Nutrition: Calories: 322 Fat: 18g Carb: 34g Protein: 9g

22. Alkaline Electric Veggie Lasagna

Preparation Time: 1 hour

Cooking Time: 70 minutes

Servings: 6

Ingredients:

- Pasta:
- Spelt lasagna sheets as needed
- Meat alternative:
- 1 tsp. fennel powder
- 2 tsp. basil
- 2 tsp. oregano
- 1 tbsp. sea salt
- 2 tbsp. onion powder
- ½ cup tomato sauce
- 1 cup red peppers, diced
- 1 cup onions, chopped
- 1 cup cooked chickpeas/garbanzo beans
- 2 cups cooked spelt berries/kernels
- Brazil Nut Cheese
- 1 tsp. basil
- 1 tsp. oregano
- 1 tsp. sea salt
- 1 tbsp. onion powder

- 1 tbsp. hemp seeds
- 1 cup spring water
- 2 cups-soaked Brazil nuts
- Extras:
- White mushrooms
- Grapeseed oil as needed
- Zucchini as needed

Directions:

1. Combine all the meat alternatives in a food processor and blend until mixed. Grease a skillet using grapeseed oil and heat over medium heat. Sauté peppers and onions for 5 minutes.

2. Add the garbanzo and spelt mixture from the food processor. Put some grapeseed oil in the skillet and cook the mixture for 10 to 12 minutes.

3. In a blender, add the cheese Ingredients and 1 cup of water and process until smooth. Reserve a cup of tomato sauce and then pour the rest of the sauce into the garbanzo bean and spelt mixture. Mix.

4. Slice the zucchini and mushrooms lengthwise. Coat the bottom of the dish using the reserved tomato sauce.

5. Then lay the spelt pasta, sliced zucchini, the garbanzo/spelt mixture, alkaline cheese, white mushrooms, and spelt pasta again.

6. Repeat until you get 4 layers of the pasta. Then top the last layer with the garbanzo/spelt mixture and cheese.

7. Pour the rest of the tomato sauce around the lasagna layers and sprinkle with some dried basil. Bake at 350F for 35 to 45 minutes. Cool and serve.

Nutrition: Calories: 575 Fat: 36g Carb: 60g Protein: 11.5g

SNACKS

23. Whole-Wheat Biscuits

Preparation time: 15 minutes

Cooking time: 12 minutes

Servings: 12-14

Ingredients:

- 1 cup all-purpose flour
- 1 cup whole-wheat flour
- 4 teaspoons baking powder
- ¼ teaspoon salt
- 1/3 cup vegan margarine/coconut oil, softened but not melted
- ¾ cup nondairy milk

Directions:

1. Warm oven to 450°F with a rack in the top position.
2. Combine the all-purpose and whole-wheat flours, baking powder, and salt in a large bowl. Sift the ingredients or mix together with a fork.
3. Add the margarine, and, using your clean fingers, mix it in until the mixture looks like coarse crumbs.

4. Add the milk, stirring with a fork or your hands until just blended (don't stir too much). Pull out pieces of the batter, about ¼ cup or so, and place them on a rimmed baking sheet, spaced at least 1 inch apart.

5. Bake for about 12 minutes, until slightly browned at the edges. Serve.

Nutrition: Calories: 169 Protein: 5g Fat: 6g Carbohydrates: 26g

24. Strawberry Milkshake

Preparation time: 5 minutes

Cooking time: 0 minutes

Servings: 1

Ingredients:

- 2 cups hulled strawberries
- 1 cup nondairy milk
- ½ cup plain nondairy yogurt or canned coconut milk
- 1 tablespoon sugar, maple syrup, or Simple Syrup (optional)
- Ice cubes, for blending (optional)

Directions:

1. In a blender, combine the strawberries, milk, yogurt, sugar (if using), and ice (if using). Purée until smooth and creamy.

Nutrition: Calories: 268 Protein: 6g Fat: 6g Carbohydrates: 51g

25. Cranberry-Oat Energy Bites

Preparation time: 15 minutes

Cooking time: 0 minutes

Servings: 12

Ingredients:

- ¾ cup rolled oats
- ¼ cup plant-based protein powder, coconut flour, or ground almonds
- 2 tablespoons dried cranberries
- ¼ cup maple syrup or Simple Syrup
- 2 to 3 tablespoons nondairy milk

Directions:

1. Prepare a small baking sheet lined using parchment paper, set aside. In a large bowl, stir together the oats, protein powder, and cranberries.
2. Add the maple syrup and stir to combine. Stir in the milk, 1 tablespoon at a time, until the mixture forms a ball when pressed together.
3. Divide the batter into 12 portions, then firmly roll each into a ball. Place them on the prepared baking sheet and refrigerate, if you can, to set for about 15 minutes.

4. Store leftovers in an airtight container in the refrigerator for up to 1 week.

Nutrition: Calories: 63 Protein: 3g Fat: 1g Carbohydrates: 12g

26. Peanut Butter–Mocha Energy Bites

Preparation time: 45 minutes

Cooking time: 0 minutes

Servings: 12

Ingredients:

- ¼ cup creamy peanut butter
- 2 tablespoons maple syrup or Simple Syrup
- 1 tablespoon nondairy milk or water, plus more as needed
- 1 to 2 teaspoons instant coffee powder or chopped roasted coffee beans (optional)
- 2 tablespoons sugar
- 2 tablespoons unsweetened cocoa powder
- 1 tablespoon ground flaxseed
- ½ cup cooked quinoa
- 2 tablespoons plant-based protein powder, coconut flour, or ground almonds

Directions:

1. Stir the peanut butter, maple syrup, and milk in a large bowl until smooth. Add the coffee powder (if using), sugar, cocoa powder, and flaxseed, stir to combine.
2. Stir in the quinoa and protein powder. Drizzle in another tablespoon of milk to moisten, if needed.

3. Divide the mixture into about 12 portions, and roll each into a small ball. Place them on a plate and refrigerate, if you can, for 30 minutes.

4. They will keep in an airtight container in the refrigerator for up to 1 week. If you don't have a fridge, enjoy them the same day.

Nutrition: Calories: 70 Protein: 3g Fat: 3g Carbohydrates: 8g

27. Cinnamon Chickpea Energy Bites

Preparation time: 35 minutes

Cooking time: 0 minutes

Servings: 16

Ingredients:

- ¾ cup canned chickpeas, drained and rinsed
- 1/3 cup unsweetened shredded coconut
- ¼ cup packed dark brown sugar, + more as needed
- 1 teaspoon ground cinnamon or pumpkin pie spice
- 2 tablespoons vegan dark chocolate chips

Directions:

1. In a food processor, combine the chickpeas, coconut, brown sugar, and cinnamon. Purée until smooth, stopping to scrape down the sides of the bowl as needed. Taste for sweetness.
2. If it still tastes "beany," add more brown sugar, 2 tablespoons at a time, until you like the taste. Pulse to combine.
3. Put the chocolate chips then pulse within a few times to mix them in and chop them a bit. Divide the batter into 16 portions, and form each into a small ball.

4. Place them on a plate and refrigerate, if you can, for 20 minutes. Serve.

Nutrition: Calories: 62 Protein: 1g Fat: 4g Carbohydrates: 7g

VEGETABLES

28. Garlicky Red Wine Mushrooms

Preparation Time: 10 minutes

Cooking Time: 15 minutes

Serving: 4

Ingredient:

- 3 tablespoons olive oil
- 2 cups sliced mushrooms
- 3 garlic cloves, minced
- ½ cup red wine
- 1 tablespoon dried thyme

Direction

1. Cook olive oil over medium-high heat until it shimmers. Mix in the mushrooms and sit, untouched, until they release their liquid and begin to brown, about 5 minutes. Stir the mushrooms occasionally, cooking until softened and golden brown, about 5 minutes more. Cook garlic. Add the red wine and thyme, using a wooden spoon to scrape any browned bits off the pan's bottom.

2. Adjust heat to medium. Cook for 5 minutes. Season well and serve.

Nutrition: 98 Calories 4g Fiber 6g Protein

29. Sautéed Citrus Spinach

Preparation Time: 10 minutes

Cooking Time: 10 minutes

Serving: 4

Ingredient:

- 2 tablespoons olive oil
- 1 shallot, chopped
- 2 garlic cloves, minced
- 10 ounces' baby spinach
- Zest and juice of 1 orange

Direction

1. Cook olive oil over medium-high heat. Cook the shallot for 3 minutes. Cook garlic for 30 seconds.
2. Add the spinach, orange juice, and orange zest. Cook for 2 minutes. Season with salt and pepper. Serve warm.

Nutrition: 91 Calories 4g Fiber 7g Protein

SALAD

30. Super Summer Salad

Preparation Time: 10 minutes

Cooking Time: 0 minutes

Servings: 2

Ingredients:

- Dressing:
- 1 tbsp. olive oil
- ¼ cup chopped basil
- 1 tsp. lemon juice
- ¼ tsp Salt
- 1 medium avocado, halved, diced
- ¼ cup water
- Salad:
- ¼ cup dry chickpeas
- ¼ cup dry red kidney beans
- 4 cups raw kale, shredded
- 2 cups Brussel sprouts, shredded
- 2 radishes, thinly sliced
- 1 tbsp. walnuts, chopped
- 1 tsp. flax seeds

- Salt and pepper to taste

Directions:

1. Prepare the chickpeas and kidney beans according to the method.
2. Soak the flax seeds according the method, and then drain excess water.
3. Prepare the dressing by adding the olive oil, basil, lemon juice, salt, and half of the avocado to a food processor or blender, and pulse on low speed.
4. Keep adding small amounts of water until the dressing is creamy and smooth.
5. Transfer the dressing to a small bowl and set it aside.
6. Combine the kale, Brussel sprouts, cooked chickpeas, kidney beans, radishes, walnuts, and remaining avocado in a large bowl and mix thoroughly.
7. Store the mixture, or, serve with the dressing and flax seeds, and enjoy!

Nutrition: Calories 266 Total Fat 26.6g Saturated Fat 5.1g Cholesterol 0mg Sodium 298mg Total Carbohydrate 8.8g Dietary Fiber 6.8g Total Sugars 0.6g Protein 2g Vitamin D 0mcg Calcium 19mg Iron 1mg Potassium 500mg

GRAINS

31. Ritzy Fava Bean Ratatouille

Preparation Time: 15 minutes

Cooking Time: 40 minutes

Servings: 4

Ingredients:

- 1 medium red onion, peeled and thinly sliced
- 2 tablespoons low-sodium vegetable broth
- 1 large eggplant, stemmed and cut into ½-inch dice
- 1 red bell pepper, seeded and diced
- 2 cups cooked fava beans
- 2 Roma tomatoes, chopped
- 1 medium zucchini, diced
- 2 cloves garlic, peeled and finely chopped
- ¼ cup finely chopped basil
- Salt, to taste (optional)
- Ground black pepper, to taste

Directions:

1. Add the onion to a saucepan and sauté for 7 minutes or until caramelized.

2. Add the vegetable broth, eggplant and red bell pepper to the pan and sauté for 10 more minutes.

3. Add the fava beans, tomatoes, zucchini, and garlic to the pan and sauté for an additional 5 minutes.

4. Reduce the heat to medium-low. Put the pan lid on and cook for 15 minutes or until the vegetables are soft. Stir the vegetables halfway through.

5. Transfer them onto a large serving plate. Sprinkle with basil, salt (if desired), and black pepper before serving.

Nutrition: calories: 114 fat: 1.0g carbs: 24.2g protein: 7.4gfiber: 10.3g

32. Peppers and Black Beans with Brown Rice

Preparation Time: 15 minutes

Cooking Time: 20 minutes

Servings: 4

Ingredients:

- 2 jalapeño peppers, diced
- 1 red bell pepper, seeded and diced
- 1 medium yellow onion, peeled and diced
- 2 tablespoons low-sodium vegetable broth
- 1 teaspoon toasted and ground cumin seeds
- 1½ teaspoons toasted oregano
- 5 cloves garlic, peeled and minced
- 4 cups cooked black beans
- Salt, to taste (optional)
- Ground black pepper, to taste
- 3 cups cooked brown rice
- 1 lime, quartered
- 1 cup chopped cilantro

Directions:

1. Add the jalapeño peppers, bell pepper, and onion to a saucepan and sauté for 7 minutes or until the onion is well browned and caramelized.

2. Add vegetable broth, cumin, oregano, and garlic to the pan and sauté for 3 minutes or until fragrant.

3. Add the black beans and sauté for 10 minutes or until the vegetables are tender. Sprinkle with salt (if desired) and black pepper halfway through.

4. Arrange the brown rice on a platter, then top with the cooked vegetables. Garnish with lime wedges and cilantro before serving.

Nutrition: calories: 426 fat: 2.6g carbs: 82.4g protein: 20.2g fiber: 19.5g

LEGUMES

33. Anasazi Bean and Vegetable Stew

Preparation Time: 10 minutes

Cooking Time: 10 minutes

Servings: 4

Ingredients:

- 1 cup Anasazi beans, soaked overnight and drained
- 3 cups roasted vegetable broth
- 1 bay laurel
- 1 thyme sprig, chopped
- 1 rosemary sprig, chopped
- 3 tablespoons olive oil
- 1 large onion, chopped
- 2 celery stalks, chopped
- 2 carrots, chopped
- 2 bell peppers, seeded and chopped
- 1 green chili pepper, seeded and chopped
- 2 garlic cloves, minced
- Sea salt and ground black pepper, to taste
- 1 teaspoon cayenne pepper
- 1 teaspoon paprika

Directions

1. In a saucepan, bring the Anasazi beans and broth to a boil. Once boiling, turn the heat to a simmer. Add in the bay laurel, thyme and rosemary; let it cook for about 50 minutes or until tender.
2. Meanwhile, in a heavy-bottomed pot, heat the olive oil over medium-high heat. Now, sauté the onion, celery, carrots and peppers for about 4 minutes until tender.
3. Add in the garlic and continue to sauté for 30 seconds more or until aromatic.
4. Add the sautéed mixture to the cooked beans. Season with salt, black pepper, cayenne pepper and paprika.
5. Continue to simmer, stirring periodically, for 10 minutes more or until everything is cooked through. Bon appétit!

Nutrition: Calories: 444; Fat: 15.8g; Carbs: 58.2g; Protein: 20.2g

34. Easy and Hearty Shakshuka

Preparation Time: 10 minutes

Cooking Time: 10 minutes

Servings: 4

Ingredients:

- 2 tablespoons olive oil
- 1 onion, chopped
- 2 bell peppers, chopped
- 1 poblano pepper, chopped
- 2 cloves garlic, minced
- 2 tomatoes, pureed
- Sea salt and black pepper, to taste
- 1 teaspoon dried basil
- 1 teaspoon red pepper flakes
- 1 teaspoon paprika
- 2 bay leaves
- 1 cup chickpeas, soaked overnight, rinsed and drained
- 3 cups vegetable broth
- 2 tablespoons fresh cilantro, roughly chopped

Directions

1. Heat the olive oil in a saucepan over medium heat. Once hot, cook the onion, peppers and garlic for about 4 minutes, until tender and aromatic.

2. Add in the pureed tomato tomatoes, sea salt, black pepper, basil, red pepper, paprika and bay leaves.
3. Turn the heat to a simmer and add in the chickpeas and vegetable broth. Cook for 45 minutes or until tender.
4. Taste and adjust seasonings. Spoon your Shakshuka into individual bowls and serve garnished with the fresh cilantro. Bon appétit!

Nutrition: Calories: 324; Fat: 11.2g; Carbs: 42.2g; Protein: 15.8g

BREAD & PIZZA

35. Coco-Cilantro Flatbread

Preparation time: 10 minutes

Cooking time: 15 minutes

Servings: 6

Ingredients:

- 1/2 cup Coconut Flour
- 2 tablespoons Flax Meal
- 1/4 teaspoon Baking Soda
- 1 tablespoon Coconut Oil
- 2 tablespoons Chopped Cilantro
- 1/4 teaspoon salt
- 1 cup Lukewarm Water

Directions:

1. In a medium bowl, whisk together the coconut flour, flax, baking soda, and salt.
2. Add in the water, coconut oil, and chopped cilantro.
3. Knead until everything comes together into a smooth dough.
4. Leave to rest for about 15 minutes.
5. Divide the dough into 6 equal-sized portions.

6. Roll each portion into a ball, then flatten with a rolling pin in between sheets of parchment paper.
7. Refrigerate until ready to use.
8. To cook, heat in a non-stick pan for 2-3 minutes per side.

Nutrition: Calories 46 Carbohydrates 1 g Fats 4 g Protein 1 g

36. Avocado Flatbread

Preparation time: 25 minutes

Cooking time: 5 minutes

Servings: 6

Ingredients:

- 130 grams Mashed Avocado
- 3/4 cup Chickpea Flour
- 1 teaspoon Cumin Powder
- 1/2 teaspoon Salt

Directions:

1. Combine all ingredients in a bowl. Stir until mixture comes together into a dough.
2. Knead the dough briefly on a lightly floured surface.
3. Leave the dough to rest for 15 minutes.
4. Divide the dough into four portions.
5. Take each portion of dough and flatten with a rolling pin.
6. Toast flatbread in a lightly oiled skillet for about 2 minutes per side.

Nutrition: Calories 80 Carbohydrates 8 g Fats 4 g Protein 3 g

SOUP AND STEW

37. Moroccan Vermicelli Vegetable Soup

Preparation Time: 5 minutes

Cooking Time: 35 minutes

Servings: 4 to 6

Ingredients:

- 1 tablespoon olive oil
- 1 small onion, chopped
- 1 large carrot, chopped
- 1 celery rib, chopped
- 3 small zucchinis, cut into 1/4-inch dice
- 1 (28-ounce) can diced tomatoes, drained
- 2 tablespoons tomato paste
- 11/2 cups cooked or 1 (15.5-ounce) can chickpeas, drained and rinsed
- 2 teaspoons smoked paprika
- 1 teaspoon ground cumin
- 1 teaspoon za'atar spice (optional)
- 1/4 teaspoon ground cayenne
- 6 cups vegetable broth, homemade (see light vegetable broth) or store-bought, or water

- Salt
- 4 ounces' vermicelli
- 2 tablespoons minced fresh cilantro, for garnish

Directions:

1. In a large soup pot, heat the oil over medium heat. Add the onion, carrot, and celery. Cover and cook until softened, about 5 minutes. Stir in the zucchini, tomatoes, tomato paste, chickpeas, paprika, cumin, za'atar, and cayenne.

2. Add the broth and salt to taste. Bring to a boil, then reduce heat to low and simmer, uncovered, until the vegetables are tender, about 30 minutes.

3. Shortly before serving, stir in the vermicelli and cook until the noodles are tender, about 5 minutes. Ladle the soup into bowls, garnish with cilantro, and serve.

Nutrition: Calories: 236 kcal Fat: 1.8g Carbs: 48.3g Protein: 7g

38. Moroccan Vegetable Stew

Preparation Time: 5 minutes

Cooking Time: 35 minutes

Servings: 4

Ingredients:

- 1 tablespoon olive oil
- 2 medium yellow onions, chopped
- 2 medium carrots, cut into 1/2-inch dice
- 1/2 teaspoon ground cumin
- 1/2 teaspoon ground cinnamon or allspice
- 1/2 teaspoon ground ginger
- 1/2 teaspoon sweet or smoked paprika
- 1/2 teaspoon saffron or turmeric
- 1 (14.5-ounce) can diced tomatoes, undrained
- 8 ounces' green beans, trimmed and cut into 1-inch pieces
- 2 cups peeled, seeded, and diced winter squash
- 1 large russet or other baking potato, peeled and cut into 1/2-inch dice
- 11/2 cups vegetable broth
- 11/2 cups cooked or 1 (15.5-ounce) can chickpeas, drained and rinsed
- ¾ cup frozen peas

- 1/2 cup pitted dried plums (prunes)
- 1 teaspoon lemon zest
- Salt and freshly ground black pepper
- 1/2 cup pitted green olives
- 1 tablespoon minced fresh cilantro or parsley, for garnish
- 1/2 cup toasted slivered almonds, for garnish

Directions:

1. In a large saucepan, heat the oil over medium heat. Add the onions and carrots, cover, and cook for 5 minutes. Stir in the cumin, cinnamon, ginger, paprika, and saffron. Cook, uncovered, stirring, for 30 seconds.

2. Add the tomatoes, green beans, squash, potato, and broth and bring to a boil. Reduce heat to low, cover, and simmer until the vegetables are tender, about 20 minutes.

3. Add the chickpeas, peas, dried plums, and lemon zest. Season with salt and pepper to taste. Stir in the olives and simmer, uncovered, until the flavors are blended, about 10 minutes. Sprinkle with cilantro and almonds and serve immediately.

Nutrition: Calories: 71 kcal Fat: 2.8g Carbs: 9.8g Protein: 3.7g

SAUCES, DRESSINGS & DIP

39. Spiced Almond Butter

Preparation time: 10 minutes

Cooking time: 5 minutes

Servings: 10

Ingredients:

- 2 cups raw almond
- 1/8teaspoon allspice
- 1/8teaspoon cinnamon
- 1/8 teaspoon cardamom
- 1/8teaspoon ground ginger
- 1/8 teaspoon ground cloves
- 1/2 teaspoon salt

Directions:

1. Place all **Ingredients:** in a food processor and blend until a smooth consistency is achieved.

2. Makes a delicious fruit and veggie dip and can be added to smoothies, on toast, on pancakes and waffles.

Nutrition: Total fat: 9.5g Cholesterol: 0mg Sodium: 117mg Total carbohydrates: 4.1g Dietary fiber: 2.4g Protein: 4g

40. Keto Strawberry Jam

Preparation time: 25 minutes

Cooking time: 5 minutes

Servings: 18

Ingredients:

- 1 cup fresh strawberries, chopped
- 1 tablespoon lemon juice
- 4 teaspoon xylitol
- 1 tablespoon water

Directions:

1. Add all **Ingredients:** to a small saucepan and place over medium heat. Stir to combine and cook for about 15 minutes. Stir occasionally.

2. After 15 minutes are up, mash-up strawberries with a potato masher or fork.

3. Pour into a heat-safe container such as a mason jar.

4. Allow to cool then cover with a lid and refrigerate. Can be stored in the refrigerator for up to 3 days. Goes great with toast and sweet sandwiches.

Nutrition: Total fat: 0g Cholesterol: 0mg Sodium: 0mg Total carbohydrates: 1g Dietary fiber: 0.2g Protein: 0.1g

APPETIZER

41. __Guacamole__

Preparation Time: 15 minutes

Cooking Time: 10 minutes

Servings: 8 servings

Ingredients:

- 2 avocados, ripe
- 1 tablespoon lime juice
- 1 cup cilantro, roughly chopped
- ½ cup red onion, roughly chopped
- ½ cup cherry tomatoes, quartered (optional)
- ¼ cup canned jalapeño peppers, chopped
- ¼ teaspoon garlic powder
- ¼ teaspoon cumin
- ½ teaspoon salt

Directions:

1. Add onion, tomato, jalapeño peppers, and lime juice to a mixing bowl. Sprinkle in all seasonings and stir to incorporate.

2. Fold in avocado chunks. Stir, but do not over-mix, to create a thick texture. Serve immediately over a salad, as a side, with vegetables, or with crackers.

Nutrition: Calories 110 Fat 10 g Protein 1.5 g Carbs 6 g

42. Banana Bread

Preparation Time: 1 hour and 5 minutes

Cooking Time: 10 minutes

Servings: 12

Ingredients:

- 3 bananas, ripe
- 1/3 cup applesauce, unsweetened
- ¼ cup almond milk
- 1 teaspoon vanilla extract
- 1¾ cup whole wheat flour
- 1/3 cup coconut sugar
- 2 teaspoons baking powder
- ½ teaspoon baking soda
- 1/3 cup chopped walnuts
- ¼ teaspoon salt

Directions:

1. Preheat oven to 350°F. Prepare a 9-inch loaf pan lined using parchment paper. Mash your bananas in a medium bowl until smooth. Add applesauce, vanilla, and almond milk and mix well.
2. Add in all other ingredients. Stir, but do not over-process. Pour batter into loaf pan.

3. Use a spatula to smooth the top. Bake for 50 to 55 minutes. Serve.

Nutrition: Calories 120 Fat 0.5 g Protein 2.5 g Carbs 27 g

SMOOTHIES AND JUICS

43. Basil Lime Green Tea

Preparation Time: 5 minutes

Cooking Time: 4 minutes

Servings: 8

Ingredients:

- 8 cups of filtered water
- 10 bags of green tea
- ¼ cup of honey
- A pinch of baking soda
- Lime slices to taste
- Lemon slices to taste
- Basil leaves to taste

Directions:

1. Add water, honey, and baking soda in the pot and mix. Add the tea bags and cover. Cook on High for 4 minutes. Open and serve with lime slices, lemon slices, and basil leaves.

Nutrition: Calories 32; Carbs 8g; Fat 0g; Protein 0g

44. Turmeric Coconut Milk

Preparation Time: 5 minutes

Cooking Time: 15 minutes

Servings: 8

Ingredients:

- 13.5 oz. coconut milk
- 3 cups of filtered water
- 2 tsps. turmeric powder
- 3 whole cloves
- 2 cinnamon sticks
- ½ tsp. ginger powder
- A pinch of pepper
- 2 tbsp. honey

Directions:

1. Place everything except the honey in the pot. Cover and cook on High for 15 minutes. Remove cloves and cinnamon sticks. Add honey, mix and serve.

Nutrition: Calories 42; Carbs 9g; Fat 0g; Protein 0g

DESSERTS

45. Chocolate and Raisin Cookie Bars

Preparation time: 15 minutes

Cooking time: 0 minutes

Servings: 10

Ingredients:

- 1/2 cup peanut butter
- 1 cup agave syrup
- 1 teaspoon pure vanilla extract
- 1/4 teaspoon kosher salt
- 2 cups almond flour
- 1 teaspoon baking soda
- 1 cup raisins
- 1 cup vegan chocolate, broken into chunks

Directions:

1. Combine the peanut butter, agave syrup, vanilla and salt in a mixing bowl. Gradually stir in the almond flour and baking soda and stir to combine.

2. Add in the raisins and chocolate chunks and stir again. Freeze for about 30 minutes and serve well chilled. Enjoy!

Nutrition: Calories: 267 Fat: 2.9g Carbs: 61.1g Protein: 2.2g

46. Walnut and Berry Cake

Preparation time: 15 minutes

Cooking time: 0 minutes

Servings: 8

Ingredients:

- Crust:
- 1 ½ cups walnuts, ground
- 2 tablespoons maple syrup
- 1/4 cup raw cacao powder
- 1/4 teaspoon ground cinnamon
- A pinch of coarse salt
- A pinch of freshly grated nutmeg
- Berry layer:
- 6 cups mixed berries
- 2 frozen bananas
- 1/2 cup agave syrup

Directions:

1. In your food processor, blend the crust ingredients until the mixture comes together; press the crust into a lightly oiled baking pan.
2. Then, blend the berry layer. Spoon the berry layer onto the crust, creating a flat surface with a spatula.

Transfer the cake to your freezer for about 3 hours. Store in your freezer. Bon appétit!

Nutrition: Calories: 244 Fat: 10.2g Carbs: 39g Protein: 3.8g

47. Chocolate Dream Balls

Preparation time: 45 minutes

Cooking time: 0 minutes

Servings: 8

Ingredients:

- 3 tablespoons cocoa powder
- 8 fresh dates, pitted and soaked for 15 minutes
- 2 tablespoons tahini, at room temperature
- 1/2 teaspoon ground cinnamon
- 1/2 cup vegan chocolate, broken into chunks
- 1 tablespoon coconut oil, at room temperature

Directions:

1. Add the cocoa powder, dates, tahini and cinnamon to the bowl of your food processor. Process until the mixture forms a ball.
2. Portion the batter into 1-ounce using a cookie scoop. Roll the balls and refrigerate them for at least 30 minutes.
3. Meanwhile, microwave the chocolate until melted; add in the coconut oil and whisk to combine well.
4. Dip the chocolate balls in the coating and store them in your refrigerator until ready to serve. Bon appétit!

Nutrition: Calories: 107 Fat: 7.2g Carbs: 10.8g Protein: 1.8g

48. Last-Minute Macaroons

Preparation time: 15 minutes

Cooking time: 11 minutes

Servings: 10

Ingredients:

- 3 cups coconut flakes, sweetened
- 9 ounces canned coconut milk, sweetened
- 1 teaspoon ground anise
- 1 teaspoon vanilla extract

Directions:

1. Warm your oven to 325 degrees F. Line the cookie sheets with parchment paper. Thoroughly combine all the ingredients until everything is well incorporated.
2. Use a cookie scoop to drop mounds of the batter onto the prepared cookie sheets. Bake for about 11 minutes until they are lightly browned. Bon appétit!

Nutrition: Calories: 125 Fat: 7.2g Carbs: 14.3g Protein: 1.1g

49. __Old-Fashioned Ratafias__

Preparation time: 15 minutes

Cooking time: 15 minutes

Servings: 8

Ingredients:

- 2 ounces all-purpose flour
- 2 ounces almond flour
- 1 teaspoon baking powder
- 2 tablespoons applesauce
- 5 ounces caster sugar
- 1 ½ ounces vegan butter
- 4 drops of ratafia essence

Directions:

1. Warm your oven to 330 degrees F. Line a cookie sheet with parchment paper. Thoroughly combine all the ingredients until everything is well incorporated.

2. Use a cookie scoop to drop mounds of the batter onto the prepared cookie sheet. Bake for about 15 minutes until they are lightly browned. Bon appétit!

Nutrition: Calories: 272 Fat: 16.2g Carbs: 28.6g Protein: 5.8g

50. Chocolates with Coconut and Raisins

Preparation time: 15 minutes

Cooking time: 0 minutes

Servings: 20

Ingredients:

- 1/2 cup cacao butter, melted
- 1/3 cup peanut butter
- 1/4 cup agave syrup
- A pinch of grated nutmeg
- A pinch of coarse salt
- 1/2 teaspoon vanilla extract
- 1 cup dried coconut, shredded
- 6 ounces dark chocolate, chopped
- 3 ounces raisins

Directions:

1. Combine all the fixings, except for the chocolate, in a mixing bowl. Spoon the mixture into molds. Leave to set hard in a cool place.
2. Melt the dark chocolate in your microwave. Pour in the melted chocolate until the fillings are covered. Leave to set hard in a cool place.

Nutrition: Calories: 130 Fat: 9.1g Carbs: 12.1g Protein: 1.3g

CPSIA information can be obtained
at www.ICGtesting.com
Printed in the USA
LVHW082007200421
685033LV00002B/209

9 781801 832489